WASHINGTON DC

Sarah Tieck

Big Buddy BOOKS
Explore the United States

VISIT US AT
www.abdopublishing.com

Published by ABDO Publishing Company, PO Box 398166, Minneapolis, MN 55439.

Printed in the United States of America, North Mankato, Minnesota.
062012
092012

 PRINTED ON RECYCLED PAPER

Coordinating Series Editor: Rochelle Baltzer
Contributing Editors: Megan M. Gunderson, Marcia Zappa
Graphic Design: Adam Craven
Cover Photograph: *Shutterstock*: kropic1.
Interior Photographs/Illustrations: *Alamy*: blickwinkel (p. 30), MPVHistory (p. 13); *AP Photo*: AP Photo (pp. 13, 25), Jacquelyn Martin (p. 27), Evan Vucci (p. 21); *Getty Images*: Eliot Elisofon//Time Life Pictures (p. 23); *Glow Images*: Visions of America, LLC (pp. 11, 17); *iStockphoto*: ©iStockphoto.com/aimintang (p. 11), ©iStockphoto.com/Birdimages (p. 30), ©iStockphoto.com/EdStock (p. 27), ©iStockphoto.com/eurobanks (p. 26); *Photo Researchers, Inc.*: Peter Muhlenberg (p. 30); *Shutterstock*: Antenna International (p. 30), Songquan Deng (p. 9), Steve Heap (pp. 19, 29), Lfink (p. 26), Ed Metz (p. 19), Mary Terriberry (p. 27), Vacclav (p. 5).

All population figures taken from the 2010 US census.

Library of Congress Cataloging-in-Publication Data

Tieck, Sarah, 1976-
  Washington DC / Sarah Tieck.
     p. cm.
  ISBN 978-1-61783-387-8
  1. Washington (D.C.)--Juvenile literature. I. Title.
  F194.3.T48 2013
  975.3--dc23
                        2012017507

Contents

One Nation

The United States is a **diverse** country. It has farmland, cities, coasts, and mountains. Its people come from many different backgrounds. And, its history covers more than 200 years.

Today the country includes 50 states. Washington DC is the country's **capital**. Let's learn more about its story!

Did You Know?

Washington DC became the US capital in 1800.

Washington DC is home to the White House. The US president lives and works in this building.

Washington DC Up Close

Washington DC is not part of any state. It is both a city and a **district**. The city is called Washington. DC stands for the District of Columbia.

The city has a total area of 68 square miles (176 sq km). About 600,000 people live there. The city is south of Maryland and north of Virginia. Its **metropolitan** area includes parts of these states.

WASHINGTON DC

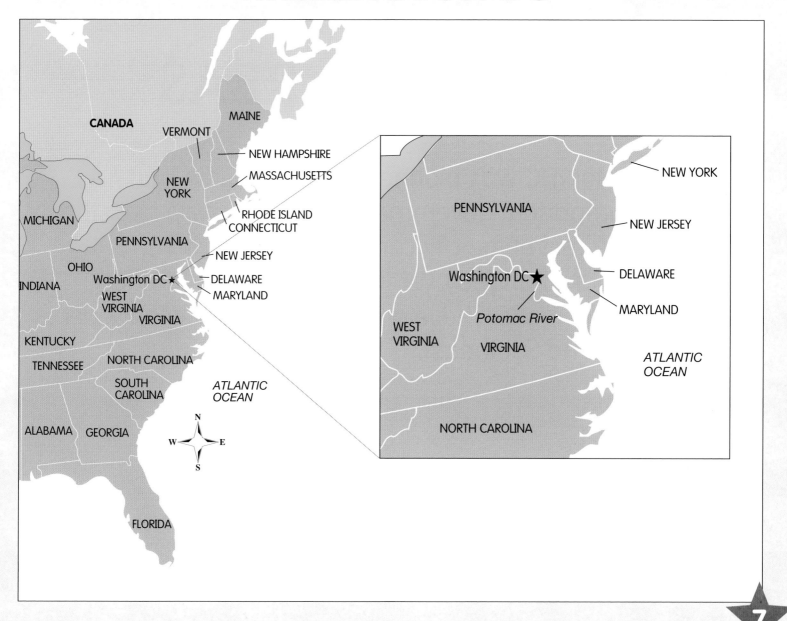

CANADA

MAINE

VERMONT

NEW HAMPSHIRE

MASSACHUSETTS

NEW YORK

RHODE ISLAND
CONNECTICUT

MICHIGAN

PENNSYLVANIA

OHIO

INDIANA

Washington DC ★

NEW JERSEY

WEST
VIRGINIA

DELAWARE
MARYLAND

VIRGINIA

KENTUCKY

TENNESSEE

NORTH CAROLINA

SOUTH
CAROLINA

*ATLANTIC
OCEAN*

ALABAMA   GEORGIA

N
W   E
S

FLORIDA

PENNSYLVANIA

NEW YORK

NEW JERSEY

Washington DC ★

DELAWARE

WEST
VIRGINIA

Potomac River

MARYLAND

VIRGINIA

*ATLANTIC
OCEAN*

NORTH CAROLINA

IMPORTANT AREAS

Washington DC was planned with four main parts. The most important government buildings were near the middle. The rest of the city centered around them.

The city has changed over time. But, it is still divided into four main parts. These are the Northwest, Northeast, Southwest, and Southeast.

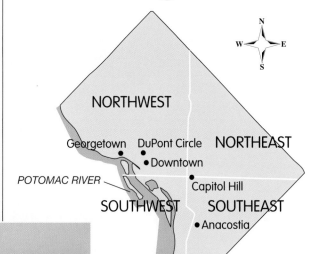

Neighborhoods in Washington DC

NORTHWEST

Georgetown DuPont Circle NORTHEAST

●Downtown

POTOMAC RIVER

Capitol Hill

SOUTHWEST SOUTHEAST

●Anacostia

Pennsylvania Avenue leads to the US Capitol near the city's center.

The Northwest is the largest section. It is home to the White House, government offices, museums, and colleges. Its famous neighborhoods include Georgetown, Downtown, and DuPont Circle.

The Northeast has many homes, parks, and gardens. The Southeast is home to parks and the Washington Navy Yard. A well-known neighborhood called Anacostia is there. The Southwest has newer buildings and government offices.

Georgetown University is in the Northwest. Well-known people have attended this college.

ANACOSTIA MUSEUM

SMITHSONIAN INSTITUTION
A MUSEUM OF AFRO-AMERICAN HISTORY & CULTURE

The Anacostia Community Museum showcases African-American history and life.

Washington DC in History

Washington DC's history includes Native Americans, explorers, and presidents. Native Americans have lived in what is now Washington DC for thousands of years. In 1608, Captain John Smith was the first European to visit.

Around 1790, president George Washington hired Pierre Charles L'Enfant to plan the US **capital**. Maryland and Virginia gave up land for it. In 1800, the capital moved from Philadelphia, Pennsylvania, to Washington DC. Since then, the city has been home to the US government.

In 1792, L'Enfant stopped planning the capital. Benjamin Banneker (*right*) helped finish his plans.

Washington DC was named for George Washington (*left*) and explorer Christopher Columbus.

Timeline

1800

Washington DC became the US **capital**. Congress moved there from Philadelphia.

1846

The Smithsonian Institution was established.

1800s

During the **War of 1812**, England's soldiers burned the US Capitol and the White House.

1814

The Washington Monument opened to the public.

1888

1963

More than 200,000 people gathered for the March on Washington. Martin Luther King Jr. gave his famous "I Have a Dream" speech.

2012

Washington DC celebrated the 100th anniversary of Japan's gift of cherry trees.

1900s

2000s

US president William Taft threw the first pitch of Washington DC's baseball season. This started the tradition of US presidents tossing the first ball.

The Washington Nationals baseball team played its first season at Nationals Park.

1910

2008

ACROSS THE LAND

Washington DC has hills, **swamps**, and rivers. The Potomac River borders the city. There are also many parks.

Theodore Roosevelt Island is a wildlife **preserve** in the city. It is home to animals such as wood ducks, woodpeckers, rabbits, and chipmunks.

Did You Know?

In July, Washington DC's average temperature is 76°F (24°C). In January, it is 32°F (0°C).

The Potomac River connects Washington DC with the Atlantic Ocean.

Earning a Living

Washington DC is the center of US government. So, thousands of people in the city work for the government! The president and Congress members are the most famous. But, other people work for the military, the courts, or other government groups.

Many people travel to Washington DC. So, the city's restaurants, hotels, parks, and museums provide lots of jobs.

Many people work at the Library of Congress (*above*), the US Capitol (*left*), and the Supreme Court (*below*).

Sports Page

Washington DC is home to several **professional** sports teams. They play baseball, basketball, football, soccer, and hockey.

College basketball has been a popular sport in this city for many years. Georgetown University and George Washington University have well-known teams.

20

The Washington Redskins
football team has many fans.

HOMETOWN HEROES

Many famous people are from Washington DC. Duke Ellington was born there in 1899. He was a jazz musician. One of his well-known songs is "It Don't Mean a Thing If It Ain't Got That Swing."

Did You Know?

Ellington began playing piano at age seven!

Ellington played piano, led a band, and wrote music.

J. Edgar Hoover was born in Washington DC in 1895. He led the Federal Bureau of Investigation (FBI) from 1924 until he died in 1972.

In the 1930s, Hoover became famous for tracking down gangsters. And, he set up the FBI's fingerprint files. Today, it is the world's largest collection.

Many of Hoover's ideas are still in use.

Tour Book

Do you want to go to Washington DC? If you visit the city, here are some places to go and things to do!

 **Play**

Take a paddleboat ride on the Tidal Basin. This is a popular way to view the city's monuments and cherry trees.

 See

Visit the National Zoological Park. It features pandas and other unusual animals.

Cheer

Catch a Washington Wizards basketball game! This team plays at the Verizon Center.

★ Remember

Check out the National Mall. This famous park is home to the Lincoln Memorial (*left*) and the Washington Monument (*right*).

Discover

Learn about US history and life at one of the Smithsonian Institution's many museums. The National Air and Space Museum features a plane flown by the Wright brothers (*left*)!

A Great City

The story of Washington DC is important to the United States. The people and places that make up this city offer something special to the country. Together with the states, Washington DC helps make the United States great.

In the spring, Washington DC is famous for its flowering cherry trees. Many people travel there just to see them bloom!

Fast Facts

Became Capital:
1800

Population:
601,723

Total Area:
68 square miles

Motto:
"Justitia Omnibus"
(Justice for All)

Postal Abbreviation:
DC

Flag:

Tree: Scarlet Oak

Flower: American Beauty Rose

Bird: Wood Thrush

Important Words

capital a city where government leaders meet.

district an area of a country or city.

diverse made up of things that are different from each other.

metropolitan of or relating to a large city, usually with nearby smaller cities called suburbs.

preserve an area set aside to keep plants and animals safe.

professional (pruh-FEHSH-nuhl) working for money rather than for pleasure.

swamp land that is wet and often covered with water.

War of 1812 a war between the United States and England from 1812 to 1815.

Web Sites

To learn more about Washington DC, visit ABDO Publishing Company online. Web sites about Washington DC are featured on our Book Links page. These links are routinely monitored and updated to provide the most current information available.

www.abdopublishing.com

Index